Sacred Values

— OF —

Gratitude Journal

SPIRIT-GUIDE'S TRAINING MANUAL

Rev. Dr. Carolyn N. Graham

BALBOA.PRESS

A DIVISION OF HAY HOUSE

Balboa Press books may be ordered through booksellers or by contacting:

Balboa Press
A Division of Hay House
1663 Liberty Drive
Bloomington, IN 47403
www.balboapress.com
844-682-1282

All Bible Scriptures Taken from the New Revised Standard Version of the Bible

Print information available on the last page.

ISBN: 978-1-9822-5302-8 (sc)
ISBN: 978-1-9822-5303-5 (e)

Balboa Press rev. date: 08/26/2020

Contents

A Note to the Spirit-Guide

This journal has several purposes, which are grounded in the belief that we have the power to change the outcomes and direction of our lives simply by the changing of our minds and our perspectives about life. This belief is underscored by sages throughout the ages. We do not begin to change the way we think without the benefit of replacing our current thoughts and beliefs with other beliefs and ideas. In other words, we replace negative, depressing, doubt with positive, affirming beliefs that are supported by a healthy vision that we have the power to design in our wonderful God-given imaginations.

This work has been designed for the benefit of young, African American people who must learn how to dream of a world where they have meaning and purpose and power. Cultivating their imagination such that it becomes creative and purpose driven will pave the way for them to design meaningful lives that can change the world.

The work requires that you, as a guide leading the training associated with this work, are focused, Spirit-driven, intentional, and relational in your guidance and work with the youth and individuals involved with the work. Prayer and meditation should always undergird your preparation prior to your encounters. You are not proselytizing or promoting any one faith walk. You are the participants' Spirit-Guide, promoting their inquiry into a Source and Force far greater than the forces of the world. Your task is to guide them to that Source whom they may choose to name by any name.

While the author of this work is a Christian by belief and training, she is also one who honors, recognizes and celebrates God's diversity in a world of many people. The youth with whom you work should be given an opportunity to know the God of many names who is known through an exploration of many paths. Your task is to start them on the journey.

The journey is a 12-month journey that begins at the beginning and ends at new beginnings as lives are transformed and visions embraced.

Learning Goals

- At the end of the process, participants will be able to describe and discuss the sacred principles and their application to their lives;
- At the end of the process, participants will design rituals, works of art, poetry, etc. that celebrate traditions that support the Sacred Values of Gratitude principles.
- Prior to each bi-weekly session, participants will have at least three days in their journal that identify lessons learned or thought about from the principle they studied, how they believe the principle applies to their life and their agreement with themselves to continue to apply them to their lives;
- At the end of each quarter, participants will demonstrate how they have incorporated the three (3) values learned during the quarter into their lives. They will design a project to present in the session as an example of what they learned.
- At the end of twelve months, each participant will present a writing or piece of art, poetry, dance, etc. about what they learned, how they feel about what they learned, and how they will use what they have learned.

As a final note, the author realizes that this is an ambitious study process. Pace the participants' study process. If all material cannot be covered in one session, do not hesitate to carry the material over to the next session.

The Twelve Sacred Values of Gratitude

Love Kindness
Faith
Understanding
Empathy
Grace
Humility
Justice
Forgiveness
Patience
Peace
Courage
Hope

Recommended Books & Materials

- ➤ A Journal: Twelve Sacred Values of Gratitude, Rev. Dr. Carolyn Graham, 2020
- ➤ A Contemporary Interpretation of the Holy Bible (e. g., The Message, New Revised Standard Version, etc.)
- ➤ the untethered soul: the journey beyond yourself, Michael A. Singer, 2007.
- ➤ Possessing the Secret of Joy, Alice Walker, 1992.
- ➤ The Gospel of Thomas: A Guidebook for Spiritual Practice, Ron Miller, 2004.
- ➤ The Journey to Spiritual Maturity: Being Salt and Light, Vol. 8, Dr. Joel C. Hunter, 2000.
- ➤ Stolen Childhood: Slave Youth in Nineteenth-Century America, 2nd Edition, Wilma King, 2011.
- ➤ The Gifts and Ministries of the Holy Spirit, Lester Sumrall, 1982
- ➤ Call to Connection: Bringing Sacred Tribal Values into Modern Life, Carole Kammen & Jodi Gold, 1998.
- ➤ Birth 2012 and Beyond: Humanity's Great Shift to the Age of Conscious Evolution, Barbara Marx Hubbard, 2012.
- ➤ Color Pencils (ample supply for doodling)
- ➤ White and color paper
- ➤ Scissors
- ➤ Elmer's glue
- ➤ Other items at the discretion of the Guide

As you begin your journey...

Three Day Cleansing Fast

As you begin your journey, I recommend that you and your students embark upon a three (3) day fast to prepare your mind, Spirit, and body for the journey.

Often our bodies become overloaded with toxins because of the foods we eat, the rest we lack, and the use of things that we use with frequency and are addicted to, e.g., coffee, sodas (sugar), candy (sugar), cigarettes, and prescribed and street drugs.

This 3-Day cleansing process will help you release toxins that have built up in your body, mind and Spirit. At its conclusion, the hope is that you will identify the path that will open you to long-term healing and ongoing health and spiritual growth. This cleansing process is recommended as the first step on your spiritual journey because we tend to resort to addictive ("ongoing use") behavior caused by the deep pain, loss, fear, emptiness, longing, etc. often so deep that it cannot be described but must be numbed-out of existence. Changes in our lives can and will come when we become realigned. This cleansing will help to support your realignment.

The path to touching the **Void Within** is important, for it is **Within the Void**—within the empty, scary, sometimes numb places that we seek to blot out the voice of Spirit is heard and known. The three-day cleanse where the body takes in lots of great water, fresh raw vegetable juices, rest and relaxation begins the healing process, which is designed to nourish the void and heal the brokenness that leads to the use of numbing additives.

Products to have on hand:

1. Water: at least two gallons of distilled or pure water. Try to drink at least eight glasses of water each day.
2. Juice: green vegetable or Carrot juice, kale, spinach, broccoli, etc. Avoid fruit juice over these 3 days.
3. Herbal tea sweetened w/honey (small jar of honey is all you will need).
4. Epsom or Himalayan Salt or other bath salt that will soften the water with a great fragrance.
5. A body brush, loofa pad, or bath pad that you can find at a pharmacy or store that has bath products.

Day 1: Friday after 6:00 pm

Around this time, take a nice relaxing bath. While in the tub, begin to tell yourself that you have already begun your healing. Sit in the tub relaxing until the water begins to cool down. Get out, dry off completely, and brush yourself with the body brush or loofa pad.

Once you have had your bath, make a hot cup of tea, sit, and just relax while sipping on your tea. Try to avoid using your phone; you will need as few distractions as you can possibly muster and agree to be separated from. Drink your tea and follow it with a big glass of water and juice. Try to journal before you go to bed. Set an intention to relax and dream. Again, stay away from the phone and texting—this is your time, do not give it to anyone!

Day 2: Saturday Morning

Rise early. Shower and wash your hair. No need to do anything to it but wash it and let it naturally dry. Read your daily meditation, reflect, and journal. Remember, no phone (except in emergencies), television (especially news). Use the time to read, meditate, journal, and quiet, thoughtful prayers.

Have a cup of hot tea; a glass of water and a glass of juice. If you are taking a detox supplement, follow the directions to take your nutrients. Drink you water and juice throughout the day. You should drink at a minimum, eight (8) glasses of water during the day, and tea as often as you want, and your vegetable juice whenever you feel hungry.

Journal: Stay away from your phone; be quite and sleep as much as you like. This is a time for resting and going within.

Follow your water, juice, tea routines throughout the day. You will have frequent trips to the bathroom, and that is great! Stay focused and ride through the discomfort that you will feel as your body releases that which it has held onto for so long. You may even feel tearful; it is okay to cry—all systems in your body are releasing and letting go.

Please use your journal as you listen to the Still Small Voice within that is calling you. Write down what you are feeling and thinking and even hearing. Sleep/nap as frequently as you like.

Play soft music, e.g., meditation, jazz, etc., as you relax, reflect, journal, read and pray. You may need to tell your mind to behave as that "other voice", your internal "roommate", may want you to give up just as you are getting deep into the process.

Take another soothing bath at the end of the day; relax and follow the brushing instructions that you used the first day and prepare for a restful night of sleep.

Day 3: Sunday

Rise early, drink your tea, water and juice, shower and put your meditation music on.

Read your daily thought teaching, Biblical Scripture or other spiritual writings, pray for guidance, and just relax.

Take your nutrients if you generally take any as they will help with your cleansing and strength and, do not forget to journal. Go through this last day as you went through day two and bring the process to a close at 6:00pm.

You will break your fast this day. Please be gentle with your body. Eat lightly, green vegetables, perhaps a piece of baked or broiled fish, and eat mindfully and intentionally—focus on what you are eating. Enjoy the Journey!

The Study Process...

Design of the Sessions

Session I: "Who Am I, and What Is My Tribe?"

Sacred Value: *Love Kindness* **Part I**

Goal: To discuss what it means to adopt a Sacred value of **"Love Kindness"** and arrive at a definition of what it looks like, what it feels like, and how it applies to participant's life.

Readings in preparation for session:

➤ Biblical Scripture: Leviticus 19:18 (New Revised Standard Version or the Message Bible)

➤ Stolen Childhood, King, Wilma, 2011
   o "In the Beginning" (Ch. 1, pgs. xvii–xxii)
   o "You Know I Am One Man That Do Love My Children" (Ch 2, pgs. 30-69)

➤ Call to Connection: Bringing Sacred Tribal Values into Modern Life, Kammen, Carole and Gold, Jodi, 1998
   o Introduction, pages 3–39

➤ "A Call To The Sacred"

➤ "A Call For Living Tribe"

Do You Know...?

To prepare for the session, study the following words and define them:

Sacred	Tribe
Love Kindness	Tradition
Gratitude	Values

In the space provided below, share your understanding of each of the above terms and be prepared to discuss in class.

1. Sacred _____

2. Love Kindness _____

3. Gratitude _____

4. Tradition _____

5. Tribe _____

6. Values _____

Each of the books identified above has a story to tell. What in your own words are the stories from each of the books shared, and how do those stories speak to you and your life?

_____

_____

_____

Session II: "Who Am I, and What Is My Tribe"

Sacred Value: *Love Kindness* **Part II**

Goal: To discuss what it means to adopt a Sacred value of "Love Kindness" and arrive at a definition of what it looks like, what it feels like, and how it applies to participant's life.

Readings in preparation for session:

➢ Biblical Scripture: Leviticus 19:18 (New Revised Standard Version, The Message Bible)

➢ Stolen Childhood, King, Wilma, 2011
   o "Us ain't never idle": The Work of Enslaved Children and Youth (Ch. 3) and
   o "When day is done": The Play and Leisure Activities of Enslaved Children and Youth (Ch 4)

➢ Call to Connection: Bringing Sacred Tribal Values into Modern Life, Kammen, Carole and Gold, Jodi, 1998
   o Introduction, pages (pg. 43-47)
   o "The First Value: Belonging" (pg. 49-65)
   o "The Second Value: Recognition" (pg. 67-82)

Do You Know...?

To prepare for the session, study the following words and define them. You previously defined these words; however you may have some new insights that can be put in the spaces below:

Reflection	Listening
Recognition	Hearing
Rescuing	

In the space provided below, share your understanding of each of the above terms and be prepared to discuss in class.

1. **Reflection** _____

2. **Recognition** _____

3. **Rescuing** _____

4. **Listening** _____

5. **Hearing** _____

Each of the books identified above has a story to tell. What in your own words are the stories from each of the books shared, and how do those stories speak to you and your life?

_____

_____

_____

Session III: "I Can Do All Things!"

Sacred Value: *Faith* **Part I**

Goal: To discuss what it means to adopt a Sacred value of "Faith" and arrive at a definition of what it looks like, what it feels like, and how it applies to participant's life.

Readings in preparation for session:

> ➤ Biblical Scripture: Luke 11:22-24 (New Revised Standard Version, The Messsage Bible)

> ➤ <u>The Journey to Spiritual Maturity: Being Salt & Light, Vol. 8</u>, Hunter, Joel C., Burton, Steve and Georgia, 2000.
>   - o "Living Beyond the Expected Limitations" (pg. 170-199)
>   - o "<u>On Being Salt and Light"</u> (pg. 202-205)

> ➤ <u>Call to Connection: Bringing Sacred Tribal Values into Modern Life,</u> Kammen, Carole and Gold, Jodi, 1998
>   - o "A Chapter from the Tribal Textbook" (pg. 108-118)
>   - o "The Fifth Value: Service" (pg. 119-139)
>   - o "The Sixth Value: Trust and Faith (pg. 141-160)

Do You Know...?

To prepare for the session, study the following words and define them:

Faith
Trust
Limitations
Salt & Light

In the space provided below, share your understanding of each of the above terms and be prepared to discuss in class.

1. **Faith** _____

2. **Trust** _____

3. **Limitations** _____

4. **Salt & Light**_____

Each of the books identified above has a story to tell. What in your own words are the stories from each of the books shared, and how do those stories speak to you and your life?

_____

_____

_____

Session IV: "I Can Do All Things!"

Sacred Value: *Faith* **Part II**

Goal: To discuss what it means to adopt a Sacred value of "Faith" and arrive at a definition of what it looks like, what it feels like, and how it applies to participant's life.

Readings in preparation for session:

➤ Biblical Scripture: Luke 11:22-24 (New Revised Standard Version, The Message Bible)

➤ The Journey to Spiritual Maturity: Being Salt & Light, Vol. 8, Hunter, Joel C., Burton, Steve and Georgia, 2000.
   o "Living Beyond the Expected Limitations" (pg. 170-199)
   o "On Being Salt and Light" (pg. 202-205)

➤ Call to Connection: Bringing Sacred Tribal Values into Modern Life, Kammen, Carole and Gold, Jodi, 1998
   o "A Chapter from the Tribal Textbook" (pg. 108-118)
   o "The Fifth Value: Service" (pg. 119-139)
   o "The Sixth Value: Trust and Faith (pg. 141-160)

Do You Know...?

To prepare for the session, study the following words and define them You previously defined these words; however, you may have some new insights that can be put in the spaces below:

Faith
Trust
Limitations
Salt & Light

In the space provided below, share your understanding of each of the above terms and be prepared to discuss in class.

1. **Faith** _____

2. **Trust** _____

3. **Limitations** _____

4. **Salt & Light**_____

Each of the books identified above has a story to tell. What in your own words are the stories from each of the books shared, and how do those stories speak to you and your life?

_____

_____

_____

Session V: "I Seek to Hear with My Heart"

Sacred Value: *Understanding* **Part I**

Goal: To discuss what it means to adopt a Sacred value of "Understanding" and arrive at a definition of what it looks like, what it feels like, and how it applies to participant's life.

Readings in preparation for session:

➤ Biblical Scripture: Psalm 118:24 (New Revised Standard Version, The Message Bible)

➤ The Journey to Spiritual Maturity: Being Salt & Light, Vol. 8, Hunter, Joel C., Burton, Steve and Georgia, 2000.
   o "Living Beyond the Expected Limitations" (pg. 170-199)
   o "On Being Salt and Light" (pg. 202-205)

➤ Call to Connection: Bringing Sacred Tribal Values into Modern Life, Kammen, Carole and Gold, Jodi, 1998.
   o "A Chapter from the Tribal Textbook" (pg. 108-118)
   o "The Fifth Value: Service" (pg. 119-139)
   o "The Sixth Value: Trust and Faith (pg. 141-160)

Do You Know...?

To prepare for the session, study the following words and define them:

Understanding	Trust
Service	Faith
Limitations	

In the space provided below, share your understanding of each of the above terms and be prepared to discuss in class. You previously defined these words, what are other definitions can you find for them? Please post below.

1. **Understanding** _____

2. **Service** _____

3. **Limitations** _____

4. **Trust** _____

5. **Faith** _____

Each of the books identified above has a story to tell. What in your own words are the stories from each of the chapters shared, and how do those stories speak to you and your life?

_____

_____

_____

Session VI: "I Seek to Hear with My Heart"

Sacred Value: *Understanding* **Part II**

Goal: To discuss what it means to adopt a Sacred value of "Understanding" and arrive at a definition of what it looks like, what it feels like, and how it applies to participant's life.

Readings in preparation for session:

- ➢ Biblical Scripture: Psalm 118:24 (New Revised Standard Version, The Message Bible)

- ➢ The Journey to Spiritual Maturity: Being Salt & Light, Vol. 8, Hunter, Joel C., Burton, Steve and Georgia, 2000.
  - o "Living Beyond the Expected Limitations" (pg. 170-199)
  - o "On Being Salt and Light" (pg. 202-205)

- ➢ Call to Connection: Bringing Sacred Tribal Values into Modern Life, Kammen, Carole and Gold, Jodi, 1998
  - o "A Chapter from the Tribal Textbook" (pg. 108-118)
  - o "The Fifth Value: Service" (pg. 119-139)

Do You Know...?

To prepare for the session, study the following words and define them. You previously defined these words; however, you may have some new insights that can be put in the spaces below:

Understanding	Trust
Service	Faith
Limitations	

1. Understanding _____

2. Service _____

3. Limitations _____

4. Trust _____

5. Faith _____

Each of the books identified above has a story to tell. What in your own words are the stories from each of the chapters shared, and how do those stories speak to you and your life?

_____

_____

_____

Session VII: "I AM Present for My Other-Self"

Sacred Value: *Empathy* **Part I**

Goal: To discuss what it means to adopt a Sacred value of "Empathy" and arrive at a definition of what it looks like, what it feels like, and how it applies to participant's life.

Readings in preparation for session:

> ➢ Biblical Scripture: Psalm 118:24 (New Revised Standard Version, The Message Bible)

> ➢ Call to Connection: Bringing Sacred Tribal Values into Modern Life, Kammen, Carole and Gold, Jodi, 1998.
>   o "A Chapter from the Tribal Textbook" (pg. 108-118)
>   o "The Fifth Value: Service" (pg. 119-139)

> ➢ The Gospel of Thomas: A Guidebook for Spiritual Practice, Miller, Ron (Translated Davis, Stevan), 2004.
>   o "Becoming A Spiritual Adult" (pg. 1-8)

Do You Know...?

To prepare for the session, study the following words and define them

Empathy	Mutual
Becoming	Faith
Other–Self	Honor

1. Empathy _____

2. Becoming _____

3. Other–Self _____

4. Mutual _____

5. Faith _____

6. Honor _____

Each of the books identified above has a story to tell. What in your own words are the stories from each of the chapters shared, and how do those stories speak to you and your life?

_____

_____

_____

Session VIII: "I AM Present to My Other-Self"

Sacred Value: *Empathy* **Part II**

Goal: To discuss what it means to adopt a Sacred value of "Empathy" and arrive at a definition of what it looks like, what it feels like, and how it applies to participant's life.

Readings in preparation for session:

> ➢ Biblical Scripture: Romans 12:10 (New Revised Standard Version, The Message Bible)

> ➢ Call to Connection: Bringing Sacred Tribal Values into Modern Life, Kammen, Carole and Gold, Jodi, 1998
>   o "The Sixth Value: Trust and Faith (pg. 141–160)

> ➢ The Gospel of Thomas: A Guidebook for Spiritual Practice, Miller, Ron (Translated Davis, Stevan), 2004
>   o "Becoming A Spiritual Adult" (pg. 1–8)

Do You Know...?

To prepare for the session, study the following words and define them. You previously defined these words; however, you may have some new insights that can be put in the spaces below:

Empathy	Mutual
Becoming	Faith
Other–Self	Honor

1. **Empathy** _____

2. **Becoming** _____

3. **Other–Self** _____

4. **Mutual** _____

5. **Faith** _____

6. **Honor** _____

Each of the books identified above has a story to tell. What in your own words are the stories from each of the chapters shared, and how do those stories speak to you and your life?

_____

_____

_____

Session IX: "Grace is the Most Powerful Force in My Life"

Sacred Value: *Grace* **Part I**

Goal: To discuss what it means to adopt a Sacred value of "Grace" and arrive at a definition of what it looks like, what it feels like, and how it applies to participant's life.

Readings in preparation for session:

> ➤ Biblical Scripture: Joel 3:18 (New Revised Standard Version, The Message Bible)
>
> Addiction & Grace: Love and Spirituality in the Healing of Addictions, May, Gerald G., M.D., 1988
>
> o "Desire: Addiction and Human Freedom" (pg. 1-20)
> o "Mind: The Psychological Nature of Addiction" (pg. 42-63
>
> ➤ The Gospel of Thomas: A Guidebook for Spiritual Practice, Miller, Ron (Translated Davis, Stevan), 2004
> o "Being a Healing Presence" (pg. 31-34)

Do You Know...?

To prepare for the session, study the following words and define them. You previously defined these words; however, you may have some new insights that can be put in the spaces below:

Grace	Desire
Human Freedom	Presence
Mind	Healing

1. Grace _____

2. Human Freedom _____

3. Mind _____

4. Desire _____

5. Presence _____

6. Healing _____

Each of the books identified above has a story to tell. What in your own words are the stories from each of the chapters shared, and how do those stories speak to you and your life?

_____

_____

_____

Session X: "Grace is the Most Powerful Force in My Life"

Sacred Value: *Grace* **Part II**

Goal: To discuss what it means to adopt a Sacred value of "Grace" and arrive at a definition of what it looks like, what it feels like, and how it applies to participant's life.

Readings in preparation for session:

> Biblical Scripture: Joel 3:18 (New Revised Standard Version, or The Message Bible)

> Addiction & Grace: Love and Spirituality in the Healing of Addictions, May, Gerald G., M.D., 1988

  o "Body: The Neurological Nature of Addiction" (pg.65–86)
  o "Spirit: The Theological Nature of Addiction" (pg. 42-63)
  o "Grace: The Quality of Mercy" (pg. 120-139)

Do You Know...?

To prepare for the session, study the following words and define them. You previously defined these words; however, you may have some new insights that can be put in the spaces below:

Grace	Desire
Human Freedom	Spirit
Mind	Healing

1. **Grace** _____

2. **Human Freedom** _____

3. **Mind** _____

4. **Desire** _____

5. **Spirit** _____

6. **Healing** _____

Each of the books identified above has a story to tell. What in your own words are the stories from each of the chapters shared, and how do those stories speak to you and your life?

_____

_____

_____

Session XI: "With Humility, I Accept the Light that Indwells Me"

Sacred Value: *Humility* **Part I**

Goal: To discuss what it means to adopt a Sacred value of "Humility" and arrive at a definition of what it looks like, what it feels like, and how it applies to participant's life.

Readings in preparation for session:

> ➤ Biblical Scripture: Luke 11:36 (New Revised Standard Version, The Message Bible)

> ➤ Urgings of the Heart: A Spirituality of Integration, Au, Wilkie and Cannon, Noreen, 1995.
> - o "The Abandoned Self: The Shadow and Holiness" (pg. 24–42)

> ➤ A Portrait of Jesus, Girzone, Joseph F., 1998
> - o "A Humble, Casual Savior?" (pg. 46–82)

Do You Know...?

To prepare for the session, study the following words and define them. You previously defined these words; however, you may have some new insights that can be put in the spaces below:

Grace	Desire
Human Freedom	Spirit
Mind	Healing

1. Grace _____

2. Human Freedom _____

3. Mind _____

4. Desire _____

5. Spirit _____

6. Healing _____

Each of the books identified above has a story to tell. What in your own words are the stories from each of the chapters shared, and how do those stories speak to you and your life?

_____

_____

_____

Session XII: "With Humility, I Accept the Light that Indwells Me"

Sacred Value: *Humility* **Part II**

Goal: To discuss what it means to adopt a Sacred value of "Humility" and arrive at a definition of what it looks like, what it feels like, and how it applies to participant's life.

Readings in preparation for session:

> ➤ Biblical Scripture: Luke 11:36 (New Revised Standard Version)

> ➤ Urgings of the Heart: A Spirituality of Integration, Au, Wilkie and Cannon, Noreen, 1995.
>   o "The Abandoned Self: The Shadow and Holiness" (pg. 24-42)

> ➤ A Portrait of Jesus, Girzone, Joseph F., 1998.
>   o "A Humble, Casual Savior?" (pg. 46-82)

Do You Know...?

To prepare for the session, study the following words and define them. You previously defined these words; however, you may have some new insights that can be put in the spaces below:

Grace	Holiness
Shadow	Spirit
Mind	Heart

1. **Grace** _____

2. **Shadow** _____

3. **Mind** _____

4. **Holiness** _____

5. **Spirit** _____

6. **Heart** _____

Each of the books identified above has a story to tell. What in your own words are the stories from each of the chapters shared, and how do those stories speak to you and your life?

_____

_____

_____

Session XIII: "Speak to My Heart About What is Right & Just"

Sacred Value: *Justice* **Part I**

Goal: To discuss what it means to adopt a Sacred value of "Justice" and arrive at a definition of what it looks like, what it feels like, and how it applies to participant's life.

Readings in preparation for session:

➢ Biblical Scripture: Isaiah 30:21 (New Revised Standard Version, The Message Bible)

➢ the untethered soul:the journey beyond yourself, Singer, Michael A.
  o "your inner roommate" (pg. 15–22)
  o "who are you?" (pg. 23–29)
  o "the lucid self" (pg. 31–38)

Do You Know...?

To prepare for the session, study the following words and define them. You previously defined these words; however you may have some new insights that can be put in the spaces below:

Inner-self	Justice
Lucid	Consciousness
The way	Self

1. **Inner-Self** _____

2. **Lucid** _____

3. **The Way** _____

4. **Justice** _____

5. **Consciousness** _____

6. **Self** _____

Each of the books identified above has a story to tell. What in your own words are the stories from each of the chapters shared, and how do those stories speak to you and your life?

_____

_____

_____

Session XIV: "Speak to My Heart About What is Right & Just"

Sacred Value: *Justice* **Part II**

Goal: To discuss what it means to adopt a Sacred value of "Justice" and arrive at a definition of what it looks like, what it feels like, and how it applies to participant's life.

Readings in preparation for session:

> ➤ Biblical Scripture: Isaiah 30:21 (New Revised Standard Version, The Message Bible)

> ➤ the untethered soul:the journey beyond yourself, Singer, Michael A.
> - o "transcending the tendency to close" (pg. 59–67)
> - o "let go now or fall?" (pg. 71–79)
> - o "removing your inner thorn" (pg. 81–87)

Do You Know...?

To prepare for the session, study the following words and define them. You previously defined these words; however, you may have some new insights that can be put in the spaces below:

Thorn	Justice
Transcending	Consciousness
Tendency	Self

1. Thorn _____

2. Transcending _____

3. Tendency _____

4. Justice _____

5. Consciousness _____

6. Self _____

Each of the books identified above has a story to tell. What in your own words are the stories from each of the chapters shared, and how do those stories speak to you and your life?

_____

_____

_____

Session XV: "As I Learn to Forgive Myself, I Can Forgive My Other-Self"

Sacred Value: *Forgiveness* **Part I**

Goal: To discuss what it means to adopt a Sacred value of "Forgiveness" and arrive at a definition of what it looks like, what it feels like, and how it applies to participant's life.

Readings in preparation for session:

> ➤ Biblical Scripture: Phil. 4:13 (New Revised Standard Version, The Message Bible)

> ➤ the untethered soul: the journey beyond yourself, Singer, Michael A.
>   o "let go now or fall" (pg. 73-79)
>   o "removing your inner thorn" (pg. 81-87)
>   o "stealing freedom for your soul" (pg. 89-98)

Do You Know...?

To prepare for the session, study the following words and define them. You previously defined these words; however, you may have some new insights that can be put in the spaces below:

Freedom	Forgiveness
Thorn	Let go
Soul	Self

1. **Freedom** _____

2. **Thorn** _____

3. **Soul** _____

4. **Forgiveness** _____

5. **Let go** _____

6. **Self** _____

Each of the books identified above has a story to tell. What in your own words are the stories from each of the chapters shared, and how do those stories speak to you and your life?

_____

_____

_____

Session XVI: "As I Learn to Forgive Myself, I Can Forgive My Other-Self"

Sacred Value: *Forgiveness* **Part II**

Goal: To discuss what it means to adopt a Sacred value of "Forgiveness" and arrive at a definition of what it looks like, what it feels like, and how it applies to participant's life.

Readings in preparation for session:

> Biblical Scripture: Phil. 4:13 (New Revised Standard Version, The Message Bible)

> <u>Urging of the Heart: A Spirituality of</u> Integration, Au, Wilkie and Cannon, N., 1995.
>   o "Codependency: A Betrayal of Wholeness (pg. 43-63)
>   o **Note: Do all of the exercises starting on pages 56-63**

Do You Know...?

To prepare for the session, study the following words and define them. You previously defined these words; however, you may have some new insights that can be put in the spaces below:

Co-dependency	Center
Betrayal	Self-Image
Wholeness	People-pleasing

1. Co-dependency _____

2. Betrayal _____

3. Wholeness _____

4. Center _____

5. Self-Image _____

6. People-pleasing _____

Each of the books identified above has a story to tell. What in your own words are the stories from each of the chapters shared, and how do those stories speak to you and your life?

_____

_____

_____

Session XVII: "I Am Centered and Focused as I Patiently Wait on Divinity's Unfoldment in My Life"

Sacred Value: *Patience* **Part I**

Goal: To discuss what it means to adopt a Sacred value of "Patience" and arrive at a definition of what it looks like, what it feels like, and how it applies to participant's life.

Readings in preparation for session:

> - Biblical Scripture: Phil. 2:13 (New Revised Standard Version, The Message Bible)

> - The Gospel of Thomas: A Guidebook for Spiritual Practice, Miller, Ron, Trans. Davies Stevan, 2004.
>   - o "Marinating in Mystery" (pg. 73-75)
>   - o "Making Space for the Spirit" (pg. 91-99)

Do You Know...?

To prepare for the session, study the following words and define them. You previously defined these words; however, you may have some new insights that can be put in the spaces below:

Marinating	Space
Mystery	Gospel
Spirit	People-pleasing

1. **Marinating** _____

2. **Mystery** _____

3. **Spirit** _____

4. **Space** _____

5. **Gospel** _____

6. **People-pleasing** _____

Each of the books identified above has a story to tell. What in your own words are the stories from each of the chapters shared, and how do those stories speak to you and your life?

_____

_____

_____

Session XVIII: "I Am Centered and Focused as I Patiently Wait on Divinity's Unfoldment in My Life"

Sacred Value: *Patience* **Part II**

Goal: To discuss what it means to adopt a Sacred value of "Patience" and arrive at a definition of what it looks like, what it feels like, and how it applies to participant's life.

Readings in preparation for session:

➤ Biblical Scripture: Phil. 2:13 (New Revised Standard Version, The Message Bible)

➤ The Gospel of Thomas: A Guidebook for Spiritual Practice, Miller, Ron, Translation by Davies Stevan, 2004.
  o "Experiencing God's Reign" (pg. 101-105)
  o "God's Reign Calls for Ready Hands" (pg. 107-115)

Do You Know...?

To prepare for the session, study the following words and define them. You previously defined these words; however, you may have some new insights that can be put in the spaces below:

Reign	Thoughtful
Ready	Disciple
Kingdom	

1. **Reign** _____

2. **Ready** _____

3. **Kingdom** _____

4. **Thoughtful** _____

5. **Disciple** _____

Each of the books identified above has a story to tell. What in your own words are the stories from each of the chapters shared, and how do those stories speak to you and your life?

_____

_____

_____

Session XIX: "The Peace of the Divine Surrounds and Undergirds Me and All of Creation"

Sacred Value: *Peace* **Part I**

Goal: To discuss what it means to adopt a Sacred value of "Peace" and arrive at a definition of what it looks like, what it feels like, and how it applies to participant's life.

Readings in preparation for session:

➢ Biblical Scripture: Psalm 29:11 (New Revised Standard Version, The Message Bible)

➢ A Portrait of Jesus, Girzone, Joseph F., 1998.
  o "His Life and Image Within Us" (pg. 83-95)
  o "The Gentle Shepherd" (pg. 96-102)

Do You Know...?

To prepare for the session, study the following words and define them. You previously defined these words; however, you may have some new insights that can be put in the spaces below:

Portrait	Space
Mystery	Gospel
Spirit	People-pleasing

1. **Portrait** _____

2. **Mystery** _____

3. **Spirit** _____

4. **Space** _____

5. **People-Pleasing** _____

Each of the books identified above has a story to tell. What in your own words are the stories from each of the chapters shared, and how do those stories speak to you and your life?

_____

_____

_____

Session XX: "The Peace of the Divine Surrounds and Undergirds Me and All of Creation"

Sacred Value: *Peace* **Part II**

Goal: To discuss what it means to adopt a Sacred value of "Peace" and arrive at a definition of what it looks like, what it feels like, and how it applies to participant's life.

Readings in preparation for session:

➤ Biblical Scripture: Psalm 29:11 (New Revised Standard Version, The Message Bible)

➤ A Portrait of Jesus, Girzone, Joseph F., 1998.
  o "His Life and Image Within Us" (pg. 83-95)
  o "The Gentle Shepherd" (pg. 96-102)
  o "God in His Own Image" (pg. 103-118)

Do You Know...?

To prepare for the session, study the following words and define them. You previously defined these words; however, you may have some new insights that can be put in the spaces below:

Image	Divine
Shepherd	Authority
God	Samaritans

1. Image _____

2. Shepherd _____

3. God _____

4. Divine _____

5. Authority _____

6. Samaritans _____

Each of the books identified above has a story to tell. What in your own words are the stories from each of the chapters shared, and how do those stories speak to you and your life?

_____

_____

_____

Session XXI: "I Am Courageous in My Rising Up and My Sitting Down; My Going In and My Coming Out"

Sacred Value: *Courage* **Part I**

Goal: To discuss what it means to adopt a Sacred value of "Courage" and arrive at a definition of what it looks like, what it feels like, and how it applies to participant's life.

Readings in preparation for session:

➢ Biblical Scripture: Romans 8:31 (New Revised Standard Version, The Message Bible)

➢ Stolen Childhood: Slave Youth in Nineteenth-Century America,
   o "The Traumas and Tragedies of Slave Children and Youth" (pg. 212-231)

Do You Know...?

To prepare for the session, study the following words and define them. You previously defined these words; however, you may have some new insights that can be put in the spaces below:

Slavery	Patrollers
Slaveholders	Drivers
Overseers	Chattel

1. Slavery _____

2. Slaveholders _____

3. Overseers _____

4. Patroller _____

5. Drivers _____

6. Chattel _____

Each of the books identified above has a story to tell. What in your own words are the stories from each of the chapters shared, and how do those stories speak to you and your life?

_____

_____

_____

Session XXII: "I Am Courageous in My Rising Up and My Sitting Down; My Going In and My Coming Out"

Sacred Value: *Courage* **Part II**

Goal: To discuss what it means to adopt a Sacred value of "Courage" and arrive at a definition of what it looks like, what it feels like, and how it applies to participant's life.

Readings in preparation for session:

> ➤ Biblical Scripture: Romans 8:31 (New Revised Standard Version, The Message Bible)

> ➤ Stolen Childhood: Slave Youth in Nineteenth-Century America, King, Wilma, 2011
>> o "The Traumas and Tragedies of Slave Children and Youth" (pg. 231-261)

Do You Know...?

To prepare for the session, study the following words and define them. You previously defined these words; however, you may have some new insights that can be put in the spaces below:

Slavery	Patrollers
Slaveholders	Drivers
Overseers	Chattel

1. **Slavery** _____

2. **Slaveholders** _____

3. **Overseers** _____

4. **Patroller** _____

5. **Drivers** _____

6. **Chattel** _____

Each of the books identified above has a story to tell. What in your own words are the stories from each of the chapters shared, and how do those stories speak to you and your life?

_____

_____

_____

Session XXIII: "My Hope is Grounded in My Faith and My Vision of the Future"

Sacred Value: *Hope* **Part I**

Goal: To discuss what it means to adopt a Sacred value of "Hope" and arrive at a definition of what it looks like, what it feels like, and how it applies to participant's life.

Readings in preparation for session:

> ➤ Biblical Scripture: Romans 8:31 (New Revised Standard Version, The Message Bible)

> ➤ Call to Connection: Bringing Sacred Tribal Values into Modern Life, Kammen, Carol & Gold, Jodi. 1998

Do You Know...?

To prepare for the session, study the following words and define them. You previously defined these words; however, you may have some new insights that can be put in the spaces below:

Wheel	Symbols
Circle	Soul
Outer Tribe	Wheel

1. **Wheel** _____

2. **Circle** _____

3. **Outer Tribe** _____

4. **Symbols** _____

5. **Soul** _____

6. **Wheel** _____

Each of the books identified above has a story to tell. What in your own words are the stories from each of the chapters shared, and how do those stories speak to you and your life?

_____

_____

_____

Session XXIV: "My Hope is Grounded in My Faith and My Vision of the Future"

Sacred Value: *Hope* **Part II**

Goal: To discuss what it means to adopt a Sacred value of "Hope" and arrive at a definition of what it looks like, what it feels like, and how it applies to participant's life.

Readings in preparation for session:

> ➤ Biblical Scripture: 1 Timothy 1:1 (New Revised Standard Version, The Message Bible)

Exercise: Based on the Sacred Values you have learned and worked with, Craft a vision of your Hope for tomorrow and your future. Be as creative as you wish. You may write a poem, draw a picture, use music, whatever comes to mind is yours to share.

Spread Your Wings & Fly & Shine Like Stars in the World

In Gratitude...

Bibliography

Au, Wilkie and Cannon, Noreen: <u>Urging of the Heart: A Spirituality of Integration</u>. New York/Mahwah, NJ: Paulist Press, 1995.

Girzone, Joseph: <u>A Portrait of Jesus.</u> New York, NY: Image Books, Doubleday, 1998.

Graham, Carolyn N.: <u>A Journal: Twelve Sacred Values of Gratitude.</u> Bloomington, IN: Balboa Press A Division of Hay House, 2020.

Hunter, Joel C.: <u>The Journey to Spiritual Maturity: Being Salt and Light, Vol 8</u>. Longwood, FL: Northland, A Church Distributed, 2000.

Kammen, Carol & Gold, Jodi: <u>Call to Connection: Bringing Sacred Tribal Values into Modern Life.</u> Salt Lake City, UT: Commune-A-Key Publishing, 1998.

King, Wilma: <u>Stolen Childhood: Slave Youth in Nineteenth-Century America,</u> 2nd Edition. Bloomington & Indianapolis, IN: Indiana University Press, 2011.

Miller, Ron: <u>The Gospel of Thomas: A Guidebook for Spiritual Practice</u>. Woodstock, VT: Skylight Paths Publishing, 2004.

Singer, Michael A.: <u>the untethered soul: the journey beyond yourself</u>. Oakland, CA: New Harbinger Publication, Inc. 2007.

Printed in the United States
By Bookmasters